365 Insp

Quotes

Daily Inspirational Quotes to Have More
Happiness, Success and Fulfillment

By Xabier K. Fernao

Any perceived slight of any individual or organization is purely unintentional.

Table of Contents

Bonus (Highly Recommended)

How do you compress decades in to days? It is by learning and modelling from people who have already walked the talk and done what you want to do.

If you want to lose weight, gain the body that you so deserve, achieve self-confidence and self-esteem that you never thought you had. I have a very special offer for you.

Enter the link below to watch a **FREE** video on Tai Lopez introducing his 67 steps program. You might have seen him on his TEDx talk, YouTube Ads, Facebooks Ads, Instagram Ads or wherever it may be on the internet.

http://bit.ly/67secrets

With over 10 million followers worldwide, he has mentored directly and indirectly many students to help them achieve the health, wealth, love and happiness that they deserve. He has helped many people earn a full time income online and successfully quit their job.

http://bit.ly/67secrets

Introduction

Isn't it true that we do not need an entire book to get inspired and do something really meaningful but maybe just a few quotes that compels us to commit to taking some massive actions?

It is truly amazing how quotes can help us refocus on the positive when we are having a bad day. A good quote that we see while queuing for our coffee or while we are walking around shopping malls can uplift our spirit and trigger positive thoughts and emotions in us.

Inspirational quotes are so profound and meaningful because they not only have deep meanings, they have different meanings to every different individual. There is no context to every quotes, except than that of your own life experiences.

Maybe a quote that you'll read in the next 365 days will trigger a major event that has happened in your life. Maybe it could remind you of the hardship that you've gone to get this far. Maybe it will give you the permission to remind yourself that you're a gift and today is precious and no matter what happens, you remember that life happens for you and not to you.

The pages that follow are a collection and compilation of my favorite quotes that I use, love and paste it all around me in small post-it. These quotes are thought-provoking, fascinating and intriguing. These quotes, without a shadow of doubt, will give you courage, energy and inspiration that will support you in your day-to-day life.

This book is yours to read as you love, but I highly recommend you go deep on each and every quote and not simply scan through each one of them and think "Cool, I've seen that somewhere, next…" With that said, I encourage you to read 1 quote a day that allows you to think and relate to your own life so that you can unleash the quote's full potential to fuel up your day with wisdom, drive and energy.

Thank you,

Xabier K. Fernao

How to Get the Most Out of this book

This book has been created to work in several ways:

1) To read the book, 1 quote a day, for 365 days. This will keep you committed to a tiny action a day and build your confidence for self-discipline each and every single day.

2) To read the book from cover to cover just like any other books and get a glimpse shot of all the meaningful and insightful quotes.

3) For you to highlight the quotes that you really love and mean something to you and write them down on a post-it or anywhere that will remind you of the greatness that you already have inside of you.

4) For you to journal and write down what each quote means to you each day as you are reading 1 quote a day and this book will become your personal inspirational quotes book that mean a huge lot to you.

I'd strongly recommend you to share a quote that really means something to you on your Facebook, Instagram and Twitter and share it with your friends what the quote means to you. You live when you grow but you get fulfillment when you give.

Note: The quotes in this book are collected from many sources and time periods. Every reasonable effort has been made to correctly attribute each quote to the original author but in some cases it was impossible to find out who really said the quote. On these cases, we'll use our own judgment to determine who really said the quote first. With that, enjoy the book and remember that life is always happening for you, and never to you. It is only a matter of perspective.

365 Days of Inspirational Quotes

Day 1

The safest way to try to get what you want is to try to deserve
what you want. It's such a simple idea. It's the golden rule.
You want to deliver to the world what you
would buy if you were on the other end.
- *Charlie Munger*

Day 2

In a time of drastic change it is the
learners who inherit the future.
The learned usually find themselves
equipped to live in a world that no longer exists
- *Eric Hoffer*

Day 3

There is nothing either good or bad,
But thinking makes it so.
- *William Shakespeare*

Day 4

Life will pay whatever price you ask of it
- *Tony Robbins*

Day 5

A nation is born stoic and dies epicurean

- Will Durant

Day 6

Great spirits have always encountered violent opposition from
mediocre minds

- Albert Einstein

Day 7

Life is not about finding yourself. Life is about creating yourself.

- Lolly Daskal

Day 8

We become what we think about most of the time, and that's the
strangest secret.

- Earl Nightingale

Day 9

If you don't design your own life plan, chances are you'll fall into
someone else's plan. And guess what they have planned for you?
Not much.

- Jim Rohn

Day 10

Keep your face always toward the sunshine—and shadows will
fall behind you.

- Walt Whitman

Day 11
The power of imagination makes us infinite.
- John Muir

Day 12
I believe that if one always looked at the skies, one would end up
with wings.
- Gustave Flaubert

Day 13
People who are crazy enough to think they can change the
world, are the ones who do.
- Rob Siltanen

Day 14
Knowing is not enough; we must apply. Wishing is not enough;
we must do.
- Johann Wolfgang Von Goethe

Day 15
Whether you think you can or think you can't, you're right.
- Henry Ford

Day 16
The only limit to our realization of tomorrow will be our doubts
of today.
- Franklin D. Roosevelt

Day 17
Creativity is intelligence having fun.
- Albert Einstein

Day 18
Do what you can with all you have, wherever you are.
- Theodore Roosevelt

Day 19
For every reason it's not possible, there are hundreds of people
who have faced the same circumstances and succeeded.
- Jack Canfield

Day 20
The journey of a thousand miles begins with one step.
- Lao Tzu

Day 21
You must be the change you wish to see in the world.
- Gandhi

Day 22
Tough times never last, but tough people do.
- Dr. Robert Schuller

Day 23

Keep on going, and the chances are that you will stumble on something, perhaps when you are least expecting it. I never heard of anyone ever stumbling on something sitting down.
- Charles F. Kettering

Day 24

There is only one success: to be able to spend your life in your own way.
- Christopher Morley

Day 25

Make each day your masterpiece.
- John Wooden

Day 26

The best dreams happen when you're awake.
- Cherie Gilderbloom

Day 27

Don't count the days, make the days count.
- Muhammad Ali

Day 28

The difference between ordinary and extraordinary is that little extra.
- Jimmy Johnson

Day 29

Even if you're on the right track, you'll get run over if you just sit there.

- Will Rogers

Day 30

Everything you've ever wanted is on the other side of fear.

- George Addair

Day 31

It is never too late to be what you might have been.

- George Eliot

Day 32

The more I want to get something done, the less I call it work.

- Richard Bach

Day 33

Even if you fall on your face, you're still moving forward.

- Victor Kiam

Day 34

The price of anything is the amount of life you exchange for it.

- Henry David Thoreau

Day 35
There are no short cuts to any place worth going.
- Beverly Sills

Day 36
If you can't outplay them, outwork them.
- Ben Hogan

Day 37
Try not. Do, or do not. There is no try.
- Yoda

Day 38
Don't wish it were easier, wish you were better.
- Jim Rohn

Day 39
What the mind of man can conceive and believe, it can achieve.
- Napoleon Hill

Day 40
Every great story on the planet happened when someone
decided not to give up, but kept going no matter what.
- Spryte Loriano

Day 41

Aim for the moon. If you miss, you may hit a star.
- W. Clement Stone

Day 42

The question isn't who is going to let me; it's who is going to stop me.
- Ayn Rand

Day 43

Twenty years from now you will be more disappointed by the things that you didn't do than by the ones you did do, so throw off the bowlines, sail away from safe harbor, catch the trade winds in your sails. Explore, Dream, Discover.
- Mark Twain

Day 44

You don't have to be great to start, but you have to start to be great.
- Zig Ziglar

Day 45

The will to win, the desire to succeed, the urge to reach your full potential… these are the keys that will unlock the door to personal excellence.
- Confucius

Day 46

Perfection is not attainable, but if we chase perfection we can catch excellence.

- Vince Lombardi

Day 47

The greatest pleasure in life is doing what people say you cannot do.

- Walter Bagehotyn Rand

Day 48

Remember that not getting what you want is sometimes a wonderful stroke of luck.

- Dalai Lama

Day 49

There are two types of people who will tell you that you cannot make a difference in this world: those who are afraid to try and those who are afraid you will succeed.

- Ray Goforth

Day 50

I can't change the direction of the wind, but I can adjust my sails to always reach my destination.

- Jimmy Dean

Day 51

There will be obstacles. There will be doubters. There will be mistakes. But with hard work, there are no limits.
- Michael Phelps

Day 52

Nothing great ever came that easy.
- Kresley Cole

Day 53

The best way to predict the future is to create it.
- Peter Drucker

Day 54

It's not about time, it's about choices. How are you spending your choices?
- Beverly Abamo

Day 55

Infuse your life with action. Don't wait for it to happen. Make it happen. Make your own future. Make your own hope. Make your own love. And whatever your beliefs, honor your creator, not by passively waiting for grace to come down from upon high, but by doing what you can to make grace happen... yourself, right now, right down here on Earth.
- Bradley Whitford

Day 56

Your time is limited, so don't waste it living someone else's life.

- Steve Jobs

Day 57

Be patient with yourself. Self-growth is tender; it's holy ground.
There's no greater investment.

- Stephen Covey

Day 58

Two roads diverged in a wood, and I—I took the one less
traveled by, And that has made all the difference.

- Robert Frost

Day 59

Life is 10% what happens to me and 90% of how I react to it

- Charles Swindoll

Day 60

Every child is an artist. The problem is how to remain an artist
once he grows up.

- Pablo Picasso

Day 61

You can never cross the ocean until you have the courage to lose
sight of the shore.

- Christopher Columbus

Day 62

I've learned that people will forget what you said, people will
forget what you did, but people will never forget how you made
them feel

- Maya Angelou

Day 63

The two most important days in your life are the day you are
born and the day you find out why.

- Mark Twain

Day 64

Certain things catch your eye, but pursue only those that capture
the heart.

- Ancient Indian Proverb

Day 65

How wonderful it is that nobody needs to wait a single moment
before starting to improve the world.

- Anne Frank

Day 66

We must believe that we are gifted for something, and that this
thing, at whatever cost, must be attained.

- Marie Curie

Day 67

Challenges are what make life interesting and overcoming them
is what makes life meaningful.
- Joshua J. Marine

Day 68

There are no traffic jams along the extra mile.
- Roger Staubach

Day 69

You become what you believe.
- Oprah Winfrey

Day 70

Education costs money. But then so does ignorance.
- Sir Claus Moser

Day 71

If you do what you've always done, you'll get what you've always
gotten.
- Tony Robbins

Day 72

It's your place in the world; it's your life. Go on and do all you
can with it, and make it the life you want to live.
- Mae Jemison

Day 73

When everything seems to be going against you, remember that
the airplane takes off against the wind, not with it.

- Henry Ford

Day 74

It's not the years in your life that count. It's the life in your years.

– Abraham Lincoln

Day 75

Nothing is impossible, the word itself says, "I'm possible!

- Audrey Hepburn

Day 76

Every strike brings me closer to the next home run.

- Babe Ruth

Day 77

There is no royal road to anything. One thing at a time, all things
in succession. That which grows fast, withers as rapidly. That
which grows slowly, endures

- Josiah Gilbert Holland

Day 78

The quickest way to double your money is to fold it over and put
it back in your pocket.

- Will Rogers

Day 79

The real opportunity for success lies within the person and not
in the job.

- Zig Ziglar

Day 80

The best revenge is massive success.

- Frank Sinatra

Day 81

Life shrinks or expands in proportion to one's courage.

- Anais Nin

Day 82

Timing, perseverance, and 10 years of trying will eventually make
you look like an overnight success.

- Biz Stone

Day 83

It always seems impossible until it's done.

- Nelson Mandela

Day 84

Eighty percent of success is showing up.

- Woody Allen

Day 85

Fear is the disease. Hustle is the antidote.

- Travis Kalanick

Day 86

The most difficult thing is the decision to act, the rest is merely tenacity.

- Amelia Earhart

Day 87

Life is what happens to you while you're busy making other plans.

- John Lennon

Day 88

It is not in the stars to hold our destiny but in ourselves.

- William Shakespeare

Day 89

Learn to say 'no' to the good so you can say 'yes' to the best.

- John C. Maxwell

Day 90

Don't judge each day by the harvest you reap but by the seeds that you plant.

- Robert Louis Stevenson

Day 91

You don't get harmony when everybody sings the same note.
- Doug Floyd

Day 92

If you think you are too small to make a difference, try sleeping with a mosquito.
- Dalai Lama

Day 93

The road to success is dotted with many tempting parking spaces.
- Will Rogers

Day 94

If you want something you never had, you have to do something you've never done.
- Thomas Jefferson

Day 95

Your labor is your contribution to the miracle.
- Elizabeth Gilbert

Day 96

We did not come to fear the future. We came here to shape it.
- Barack Obama

Day 97

There is no great genius without a mixture of madness
- *Aristotle*

Day 98

The greatest thing in the world is to know how to belong to
oneself.
- *Michel de Montaigne*

Day 99

Never let the odds keep you from doing what you know in your
heart you were meant to do.
- *H. Jackson Brown Jr*

Day 100

Who looks outside, dreams; who looks inside, awakes.
- *Carl Jung*

Day 101

Paths are made by walking.
- *Franz Kafka*

Day 102

Ever tried. Ever failed. No matter. Try again. Fail again. Fail
better.
- *Samuel Beckett*

Day 103

You will become as small as your controlling desire; as great as you dominant aspiration.

- James Allen

Day 104

The only way to do great work is to love what you do. If you haven't found it yet, keep looking. Don't settle. As with all matters of the heart, you'll know when you find it.

- Steve Jobs

Day 105

Ask and it will be given to you; seek and you will find; knock and the door will be opened to you.

- Jesus

Day 106

A ship is always safe a shore but that is not what it's built for.

- Albert Einstein

Day 107

Not all those who wander are lost.

- J. R. R. Tolkien

Day 108

Some men see things as they are and ask why. Others dream things that never were and ask why not.

- George Bernard Shaw

Day 109
Life is not always a matter of holding good cards, but
sometimes, playing a poor hand well.
- Jack London

Day 110
Live your beliefs and you can turn the world around.
- Henry David Thoreau

Day 111
That which does not kill us makes us stronger.
- Friedrich Nietzsche

Day 112
Be yourself; everyone else is already taken.
- Oscar Wilde

Day 113
The wisest mind has something yet to learn.
- George Santanaya

Day 114
Failure is the condiment that gives success its flavor.
- Truman Capote

Day 115

Experience is what you get when you don't get what you want.
- *Dan Stanford*

Day 116

A happy person is not a person in a certain set of circumstances,
but rather a person with a certain set of attitudes.
- *Hugh Downs*

Day 117

If you're going to be able to look back on something and laugh
about it, you might as well laugh about it now.
- *Marie Osmond*

Day 118

Remember that happiness is a way of travel, not a destination.
- *Roy Goodman*

Day 119

If you want to test your memory, try to recall what you were
worrying about one year ago today.
- *E. Joseph Cossman*

Day 120

We judge of man's wisdom by his hope.
- *Ralph Waldo Emerson*

Day 121

The best way to cheer yourself up is to try to cheer somebody else up.

- Mark Twain

Day 122

Many great ideas go unexecuted, and many great executioners are without ideas. One without the other is worthless.

- Tim Blixseth

Day 123

The world is more malleable than you think and it's waiting for you to hammer it into shape.

- Bono

Day 124

Sometimes you just got to give yourself what you wish someone else would give you.

- Dr Phil

Day 125

Rarely have I seen a situation where doing less than the other guy is a good strategy.

- Jimmy Spithill

Day 126

There are two primary choices in life: to accept conditions as they exist, or accept the responsibility for changing them.
- Dr. Denis Waitley

Day 127

Sooner or later, those who win are those who think they can.
- Richard Bach

Day 128

Where the willingness is great, the difficulties cannot be great.
- Machiavelli

Day 129

In three words I can sum up everything I've learned about life: It goes on.
- Robert Frost

Day 130

Positive anything is better than negative thinking.
- Elbert Hubbard

Day 131

To be successful, you must accept all challenges that come your way. You can't just accept the ones you like.
- Mike Gafka

Day 132

Life is a shipwreck but we must not forget to sing in the lifeboats.

- Voltaire

Day 133

The secret to life is meaningless unless you discover it yourself.

- W. Somerset Maugham

Day 134

Have the passion, take the action & magic will happen.

- Bar Rafaeli

Day 135

Life is not about ALL the wrong moves you made, Life is about the one right move that made ALL the difference.

- James Lockhart

Day 136

Be humble enough to admit you're not perfect, but determined enough to strive to be perfect.

- Babsie Burke

Day 137

Doing the best at this moment puts you in the best place for the next moment.

- Oprah Winfrey

Day 138

If we are not ashamed to think it, we should not be ashamed to say it.

- Marcus Tullius Cicero

Day 139

Stop acting so small. You are the universe in ecstatic motion.

- Rumi

Day 140

Fortune sides with him who dares.

- Virgil

Day 141

I am in earnest. I will not equivocate; I will not excuse. I will not retreat a single inch – and I will be heard!

- William Lloyd Garrison

Day 142

Fortune sides with him who dares.

- Virgil

Day 143

There is no chance, no destiny, no fate, that can hinder or control the firm resolve of a determined soul.

- Ella Wheeler Wilcox

Day 144

BE an opener of doors.
- *Ralph Waldo Emerson*

Day 145

We can easily forgive a child who is afraid of the dark. The real
tragedy of life is when men are afraid of the light.
- *Plato*

Day 146

Warriors do not lower themselves to the standards of other
people; they live independently according to their own standards
and code of honor.
- *Bohdi Sanders*

Day 147

The outer conditions of a person's life will always be found to
reflect their inner beliefs.
- *James Lane Allen*

Day 148

Knowledge makes a man unfit to be a slave.
- *Frederick Douglass*

Day 149

It is easy to live for others, everybody does. I call on you to live
for yourself.
- *Ralph Waldo Emerson*

Day 150

When you do what you fear most, then you can do anything.
- *Stephen Richards*

Day 151

Find out what you're afraid of, and go live there
- *Chuck Palahniuk*

Day 152

Life's challenges are not supposed to paralyze you, they're
supposed to help you discover who you are.
- *Bernice Johnson Reagon*

Day 153

And the trouble is, if you don't risk anything, you risk more.
- *Erica Jong*

Day 154

When the ax came into the forest, the trees said, 'The handle is
one of us.
- *Alice Walker*

Day 155

Do not be afraid; our fate cannot be taken from us. It is a gift.
- *Dante Alighieri*

Day 156

Courage isn't having the strength to go on—it is going on when you don't have strength.

- Napoléon Bonaparte

Day 157

Life is a daring adventure or it is nothing at all.

- Helen Keller

Day 158

It is during our darkest moments that we must focus to see the light.

- Aristotle

Day 159

Everything has beauty, but not everyone can see.

- Confucius

Day 160

I attribute my success to this: I never gave or took any excuse

- Florence Nightingale

Day 161

For small creatures such as we, the vastness is bearable only through love.

- Carl Sagan

Day 162
A year from now you may wish you had started today.
- Karen Lamb

Day 163
Man is free at the instant he wants to be.
- Voltaire

Day 164
It takes a strong fish to swim against the current. Even a dead one can float with it.
- John Crowe

Day 165
Independence is happiness.
- Susan B. Anthony

Day 166
If you have knowledge, let others light their candles in it.
- Margaret Fuller

Day 167
Good is the enemy of great.
- Jim Collins

Day 168

There are two ways of spreading light: to be the candle or the mirror that reflects it.

- Edith Wharton

Day 169

A mind is like a parachute. It doesn't work if it isn't open.

- Frank Zappa

Day 170

Today a reader, tomorrow a leader.

- Margaret Fuller

Day 171

Always make a total effort, even when the odds are against you

- Arnold Palmer

Day 172

Thousands of candles can be lighted from a single candle. Happiness never decreases by being shared.

- Gautam Buddha

Day 173

A successful man is one who can lay a firm foundation with the bricks that others throw at him.

- Sidney Greenberg

Day 174

You can be the ripest, juciest peach in the world, and there are still going to be some people who hate peaches.

- Dita Von Teese

Day 175

There is no substitute for hard work, 23 or 24 hours a day. And there is no substitute for patience and acceptance.

- Cesar Chavez

Day 176

Being an optimist after you've got the very thing you want doesn't count.

- Ken Hubbard

Day 177

You know you're in love when you don't want to fall asleep because reality is finally better than your dreams.

- Dr. Seuss

Day 178

A pessimist sees the difficulty in every opportunity; an optimist sees the opportunity in every difficulty.

- Sir Winston Churchill

Day 179

May I never be complete. May I never be content. May I never be perfect.
- *Chuck Palahniuk*

Day 180

When I work fourteen hours a day, seven days a week, I get lucky.
- *Dr. Armand Hammer*

Day 181

Don't live the same year 75 times and call it a life.
- *Robin Sharma*

Day 182

Either write something worth reading or do something worth writing.
- *Benjamin Franklin*

Day 183

Everything should be made as simple as possible, but not simpler.
- *Albert Einstein*

Day 184

There will come a time when you believe everything is finished. That will be the beginning.
- *Louis L'Amour*

Day 185

The common denominator of success is in forming the habit of doing the things that failures don't like to do.

- Albert Gray

Day 186

Happiness is like a kiss. You must share it to enjoy it.

- Bernard Meltzer

Day 187

Your income is directly related to your philosophy, not the economy.

- Jim Rohn

Day 188

A hero is someone who has given his or her life to something bigger than oneself.

- Joseph Campbell

Day 189

Life is short, and the world is wide.

- Simon Raven

Day 190

People seldom do what they believe in. They do what is convenient, then repent.

- Bob Dylan

Day 191

Diligence is the mother of good luck.

- Benjamin Franklin

Day 192

All things share the same breath - the beast, the tree, the man...
the air shares its spirit with all the life it supports.

- Chief Seattle

Day 193

To climb steep hills requires a slow pace at first.

- William Shakespeare

Day 194

I'm intimidated by the fear of being average.

- Taylor Swift

Day 195

If you focus on results you'll never change. If you focus on
change, you'll get results.

- Jack Dixon

Day 196

We are what we repeatedly do. Excellence, then, is not an act,
but a habit.

- Aristotle

Day 197
Don't blame the boss. He has enough problems.
- Donald Rumsfeld

Day 198
If you don't set goals, you can't regret not reaching them.
- Yogi Berra

Day 199
You know you are truly alive when you're living among lions.
- Karen Blixen

Day 200
Optimism is the one quality more associated with success and
happiness than any other.
- Brian Tracy

Day 201
If something is important enough, even if the odds are against
you, you should still do it.
- Elon Musk

Day 202
If it scares you, it might be a good thing to try.
- Seth Godin

Day 203

Entrepreneurship is neither a science nor an art. It is a practice.

- Peter Drucker

Day 204

Pray as though everything depended on God. Work as though everything depended on you.

- Saint Augustine

Day 205

Time is what we want most, but what we use worst.

- William Penn

Day 206

The rung of a ladder was never meant to rest upon, but only to hold a man's foot long enough to enable him to put the other somewhat higher.

- Thomas Huxley

Day 207

Flaming enthusiasm, backed by horse-sense and persistence, is the quality that most frequently makes for success.

- Dale Carnegie

Day 208

Smooth seas do not make skillful sailors.

- African Proverb

Day 209

All television is educational television. The question is: what is it teaching?

- Nicholas Johnson

Day 210

The only place success comes before work is in the dictionary.

- Vidal Sassoon

Day 211

Do not indulge in dreams of having what you have not, but reckon up the chief of the blessings you do possess, and then thankfully remember how you would crave for them if they were not yours.

- Marcus Aurelius

Day 212

The history of the world is the history of a few people who had faith in themselves.

- Swami Vivekananda

Day 213

Your vision will become clear only when you look into your heart. Who looks outside, dreams. Who looks inside, awakens.

- Carl Jung

Day 214

Act as if what you do makes a difference. It does.
- *William James*

Day 215

Perseverance is the hard work you do after you get tired of doing the hard work you already did.
- *Newt Gingrich*

Day 216

Action may not always bring happiness; but there is no happiness without action.
- *Benjamin Disraeli*

Day 217

Faith is the art of holding on to things your reason has once accepted, in spite of your changing moods.
- *C.S. Lewis*

Day 218

If people knew how hard I worked to achieve my mastery, it wouldn't seem so wonderful after all.
- *Michaelengo*

Day 219

If they can make penicillin out of moldy bread, they can sure make something out of you.
- *Muhammad Ali*

Day 220

Success is often achieved by those who don't know that failure is
inevitable.

- Coco Chanel

Day 221

Age is an issue of mind over matter. If you don't mind, it doesn't
matter.

- Mark Twain

Day 222

If the wind will not serve, take to the oars.

- Latin Proverb

Day 223

Happiness is not something readymade. It comes from your own
actions.

- Dalai Lama

Day 224

Don't worry about failures, worry about the chances you miss
when you don't even try.

- Jack Canfield

Day 225

Though no one can go back and make a brand new start, anyone
can start from now and make a brand new ending.

- Carl Bard

Day 226

Always be a first-rate version of yourself, instead of a second-rate version of somebody else.

- Judy Garland

Day 227

What lies behind us and what lies before us are tiny matters compared to what lies within us.

- Henry S. Haskins

Day 228

If you cannot do great things, do small things in a great way.

- Napoleon Hill

Day 229

An obstacle is often a stepping stone.

- William Prescott

Day 230

Do what you love and the money will follow.

- Marsha Sinetar

Day 231

The dreamers are the saviors of the world.

- James Allen

Day 232

Obsessed is just a word the lazy use to describe the dedicated.
- *Russell Warren*

Day 233

I will go anywhere as long as it is forward.
- *David Livingston*

Day 234

If you aren't going all the way, why go at all?
- *Joe Namath*

Day 235

Just keep going. Everybody gets better if they keep at it.
- *Ted Williams*

Day 236

It wasn't raining when Noah built the ark..
- *Howard Ruff*

Day 237

The greatest discovery of my generation is that a human being
can alter his life by altering the attitudes of his mind.
- *William James*

Day 238

The aim of an argument or discussion should not be victory, but progress.

- Joseph Joubert

Day 239

To live is the rarest thing in the world. Most people exist, that is all.

- Oscar Wilde

Day 240

Freedom is not the absence of commitments, but the ability to choose yours.

- Paulo Coelho

Day 241

It's time to start living the life you've imagined.

- Henry James

Day 242

Every man dies. Not every man really lives.

- William Wallace

Day 243

Don't be pushed by your problems. Be led by your dreams.

- Ralph Waldo Emerson

Day 244

A compliment is something like a kiss through a veil.

- Victor Hugo

Day 245

A successful man is one who can lay a firm foundation with the
bricks others have thrown at him.

- David Brinkley

Day 246

An invincible determination can accomplish almost anything and
in this lies the great distinction between great men and little
men.

- Thomas Fuller

Day 247

Be faithful to that which exists within yourself.

- Andre Gide

Day 248

Be happy with what you have. Be excited about what you want.

- Alan Cohen

Day 249

Be patient with yourself. Self-growth is tender; it's holy ground.
There's no greater investment.

- Stephen Covey

Day 250

Can you imagine what I would do if I could do all I can?
- *Sun Tzu*

Day 251

Clouds come floating into my life, no longer to carry rain or
usher storm, but to add color to my sunset sky.
- *Rabindranath Tagore*

Day 252

Courage is doing what you're afraid to do. There can be no
courage unless you're scared.
- *Eddie Rickenbacker*

Day 253

Don't worry about the world coming to an end today. It's
already tomorrow in Australia.
- *Charles Schulz*

Day 254

Dream as if you'll live forever, live as if you'll die today.
- *James Dean*

Day 255

Everything that irritates us about others can lead us to an
understanding of ourselves.
- *Carl Jung*

Day 256

Give light and people will find the way.
- *Ella Baker*

Day 257

Give yourself an even greater challenge than the one you are
trying to master and you will develop the powers necessary to
overcome the original difficulty.
- *William J. Bennett*

Day 258

Happiness resides not in possessions, and not in gold, happiness
dwells in the soul.
- *Democritus*

Day 259

I intend to live forever. So far, so good.
- *Steven Wright*

Day 260

He who lives in harmony with himself lives in harmony with the
universe.
- *Marcus Aurelius*

Day 261

Ideas shape the course of history.
- *John Maynard Keynes*

Day 262
If everyone is thinking alike, then somebody isn't thinking.
- *George S. Patton*

Day 263
If you are going to achieve excellence in big things, you develop the habit in little matters. Excellence is not an exception, it is a prevailing attitude.
- *Charles R. Swindoll*

Day 264
If you can imagine it, you can achieve it; if you can dream it, you can become it.
- *William Arthur Ward*

Day 265
If you start to think the problem is 'out there,' stop yourself. That thought is the problem.
- *Stephen Covey*

Day 266
In the depth of winter, I finally learned that within me there lay an invincible summer.
- *Albert Camu*

Day 267
In the midst of movement and chaos, keep stillness inside of you.
- Deepak Chopra

Day 268
Intelligence is really a kind of taste: taste in ideas.
- Susan Sontag

Day 269
It is always the simple that produces the marvelous.
- Amelia Barr

Day 270
It is by acts and not by ideas that people live.
- Harry Emerson Fosdick

Day 271
Man never made any material as resilient as the human spirit.
- Bern Williams

Day 272
Nurture your minds with great thoughts. To believe in the heroic makes heroes.
- Benjamin Disraeli

Day 273

Pain is temporary. It may last a minute, or an hour, or a day, or a
year, but eventually it will subside and something else will take
its place. If I quit, however, it lasts forever.

- Lance Armstrong

Day 274

Put your heart, mind, and soul into even your smallest acts. This
is the secret of success.

- Swami Sivananda

Day 275

Reflect upon you present blessings, of which every man has
many—not on your past misfortunes, of which all men have
some.

- Charles Dickens

Day 276

Study while others are sleeping; work while others are loafing;
prepare while others are playing; and dream while others are
wishing.

- William Arthur Ward

Day 277

The art of living lies less in eliminating our troubles than
growing with them.

- Bernard M. Baruch

Day 278

The quality of a person's life is in direct proportion to their commitment to excellence, regardless of their chosen field of endeavor.

- Vince Lombardi

Day 279

The secret of joy in work is contained in one word – excellence. To know how to do something well is to enjoy it.

- Pearl Buck

Day 280

There is nothing stronger in the world than gentleness.

- Han Suyin

Day 281

Think with your whole body.

- Taisen Deshimaru

Day 282

Thought is the wind, knowledge the sail, and mankind the vessel.

- Augustus Hare

Day 283

Try to be like the turtle – at ease in your own shell.

- Bill Copeland

Day 284

We can't help everyone, but everyone can help someone.

- Ronald Reagan

Day 285

Wear your learning, like your watch, in a private pocket: and do not pull it out and strike it, merely to show that you have one

- Philip Stanhope

Day 286

Whoever is happy will make others happy too.

- Anne Frank

Day 287

Happiness is a butterfly, which when pursued, is always beyond your grasp, but which, if you will sit down quietly, may alight upon you.

- Nathaniel Hawthorne

Day 288

Your life will get better when you realize it's better to be alone than to chase people who don't really care about you.

- Thema Davis

Day 289

From every wound there is a scar, and every scar tells a story. A story that says, "I survived."

- Craig Scott

Day 290

Loneliness is not lack of company, loneliness is lack of purpose.
- Guillermo Maldonado

Day 291

There will always be a reason why you meet people. Either you
need them to change your life or you're the one that will change
theirs.
- Angel Flonis Harefa

Day 292

Life is about making an impact, not making an income
- Kevin Kruse

Day 293

Do not pray for an easy life, pray for the strength to endure a
difficult one.
- Bruce Lee

Day 294

The great thing in this world is not so much where you stand, as
in what direction you are moving.
- Oliver Wendell Holmes

Day 295

If you hear a voice within you say, 'You cannot paint,' then by all
means paint and that voice will be silenced.
- Vincent van Gogh

Day 296

Few things can help an individual more than to place
responsibility on him, and to let him know that you trust him.
- Booker T Washington

Day 297

Love is the ultimate outlaw. It just won't adhere to any rules.
The most any of us can do is sign on as its accomplice.
- Tom Watson

Day 298

Some cause happiness wherever they go; others whenever they
go.
- Oscar Wilde

Day 299

The value of an idea lies in the using of it.
- Thomas Edison

Day 300

Your most unhappy customers are your greatest source of
learning.
- Bill Gates

Day 301

Data beats emotions.
- Sean Rad

Day 302

Step out of the history that is holding you back. Step into the new story you are willing to create.

- Oprah Winfrey

Day 303

Diligence is the mother of good luck.

- Benjamin Franklin

Day 304

Risk more than others think is safe. Dream more than others think is practical.

- Howard Schultz

Day 305

However difficult life may seem, there is always something you can do and succeed at.

- Stephen Hawking

Day 306

Accept responsibility for your life. Know that it is you who will get you where you want to go, no one else.

- Les Brown

Day 307

There is no greater agony than bearing an untold story inside you.

- Maya Angelou

Day 308

A man who dares to waste one hour of time has not discovered
the value of life.

- Charles Darwin

Day 309

Today's Accomplishments Were Yesterday's Impossibilities.

- Robert H. Schuller

Day 310

Success seems to be largely a matter of hanging on after others
have let go.

- William Feather

Day 311

I owe my success to having listened respectfully to the very best
advice, and then going away and doing the exact opposite.

- G. K. Chesterton

Day 312

You have to believe in yourself when no one else does — that
makes you a winner right there.

- Venus Williams

Day 313

If you can push through that feeling of being scared, that feeling
of taking a risk, really amazing things can happen.

- Marissa Mayer

Day 314

Being Challenged In Life Is Inevitable, Being Defeated Is
Optional.
- Roger Crawford

Day 315

It is better to fail in originality than to succeed in imitation.
- Herman Melville

Day 316

When I hear somebody sigh, Life is hard, I am always tempted
to ask, 'Compared to what?
- Sydney Harris

Day 317

Remember, today is the tomorrow you worried about yesterday.
- Dale Carnegie

Day 318

If you are working on something that you really care about, you
don't have to be pushed. The vision pulls you.
- Steve Jobs

Day 319

Pleasure in the job puts perfection in the work.
- Aristotle

Day 320

Great men are not born great, they grow great.
- Vito Corleone, The Godfather

Day 321

Strength shows not only in the ability to persist, but in the ability to start over.
- F. Scott Fitzgerald

Day 322

In the end, a vision without the ability to execute it is probably a hallucination.
- Steve Case

Day 323

If you can't fly then run. If you can't run, then walk. And, if you can't walk, then crawl, but whatever you do, you have to keep moving forward.
- Martin Luther King Jr.

Day 324

A dream does not become reality through magic; it takes sweat, determination and hard work.
- Colin Powell

Day 325

Obstacles don't have to stop you. If you run into a wall, don't turn around and give up. Figure out how to climb it, go through it, or work around it.
- Michael Jordan

Day 326

I knew that if I failed I wouldn't regret that, but I knew the one thing I might regret is not trying.

- Jeff Bezos

Day 327

Everything you've ever wanted is on the other side of fear.

- George Addair

Day 328

People often say that motivation doesn't last. Well, neither does bathing – that's why we recommend it daily.

- Zig Ziglar

Day 329

The elevator to success is out of order. You'll have to use the stairs… one step at a time.

- Joe Girard

Day 330

Listen, smile, agree, and then do whatever you were gonna do anyway.

- Robert Downey Jr.

Day 331

You are not a rug…everyone may try to walk all over you, but you do not have to lie there and take it!

- Linda Poindexter

Day 332
You get what you settle for.
- *Thelma and Louise*

Day 333
Only those who will risk going too far can possibly find out how
far one can go.
- *T. S. Eliot*

Day 334
If you don't build your dream, someone else will hire you to help
them build theirs.
- *Dhirubhai Ambani*

Day 335
Don't be too timid and squeamish about your actions. All life is
an experiment. The more experiments you make the better.
- *Ralph Waldo Emerson*

Day 336
And the day came when the risk to remain tight in a bud was
more painful than the risk it took to blossom.
- *Anais Nin*

Day 337
Life is being on the wire, everything else is just waiting.
- *Karl Wallenda*

Day 338

Pearls don't lie on the seashore. If you want one, you must dive for it.

- Chinese Proverb

Day 339

The first step toward success is taken when you refuse to be a captive of the environment in which you first find yourself.

- Mark Caine

Day 340

Always go with your passions. Never ask yourself if it's realistic or not.

- Deepak Chopra

Day 341

Leap and the net will appear.

- Zen Proverb

Day 342

Life is inherently risky. There is only one big risk you should avoid at all costs, and that is the risk of doing nothing.

- Denis Waitley

Day 343

Everybody is a genius. But if you judge a fish by its ability to climb a tree, it will live its whole life believing that it is stupid.

- Albert Einstein

Day 344

The reality is: sometimes you lose. And you're never too good to lose. You're never too big to lose. You're never too smart to lose. It happens.

- Beyonce

Day 345

One of the greatest diseases is to be nobody to anybody.

- Mother Teresa

Day 346

Everything you can imagine is real.

- Pablo Picasso

Day 347

Great minds discuss ideas; average minds discuss events; small l minds discuss people.

- Eleanor Roosevelt

Day 348

It's Not Whether You Get Knocked Down, It's Whether You Get Up.

- Vince Lombardi

Day 349

You don't choose your family. They are God's gift to you, as you are to them.

- Desmond Tutu

Day 350

The true measure of a man is how he treats someone who can
do him absolutely no good
- Samuel Johnson

Day 351

The Way Get Started Is To Quit Talking And Begin Doing.
- Walt Disney

Day 352

Life is short, and it is here to be lived.
- Kate Winslet

Day 353

Move fast and break things. Unless you are breaking stuff, you
are not moving fast enough.
- Mark Zuckerberg

Day 354

I think it is possible for ordinary people to choose to be
extraordinary.
- Elon Musk

Day 355

What separates the winners from the losers is how a person
reacts to each new twist of fate.
- Donald Trump

Day 356

One good thing about music, when it hits you, you feel no pain.
- Bob Marley

Day 357

Nearly all men can stand adversity, but if you want to test a
man's character, give him power.
- Abraham Lincoln

Day 358

Trust your own instinct. Your mistakes might as well be your
own, instead of someone else's
- Billy Wilder

Day 359

Don't cry because it's over, smile because it happened.
- Dr. Seuss

Day 360

You only live once, but if you do it right, once is enough.
- Mae West

Day 361

The way I see it, if you want the rainbow, you gotta put up with
the rain.
- Dolly Parton

Day 362

I believe every human has a finite number of heartbeats. I don't intend to waste any of mine.

- Neil Armstrong

Day 363

People ask, 'What's the best role you've ever played?' The next one.

- Kevin Kline

Day 364

Identity is a prison you can never escape, but the way to redeem your past is not to run from it, but to try to understand it, and use it as a foundation to grow.

- Jay Z

Day 365

If you want to make a permanent change, stop focusing on the size of your problems and start focusing on the size of you!

- T. Harv Eker

Bonus (Highly Recommended)

How do you compress decades in to days? It is by learning and modelling from people who have already walked the talk and done what you want to do.

If you want to lose weight, gain the body that you so deserve, achieve self-confidence and self-esteem that you never thought you had. I have a very special offer for you.

Enter the link below to watch a **FREE** video on Tai Lopez introducing his 67 steps program. You might have seen him on his TEDx talk, YouTube Ads, Facebooks Ads, Instagram Ads or wherever it may be on the internet.

http://bit.ly/67secrets

With over 10 million followers worldwide, he has mentored directly and indirectly many students to help them achieve the health, wealth, love and happiness that they deserve. He has helped many people earn a full time income online and successfully quit their job.

http://bit.ly/67secrets

Conclusion

Guess what? You've made it! Yes! You've completed this book and you've done what majority of people would never do! Did you know that less than 10 percent of people who buy a book read past the first chapter? What an unbelievable waste! This is a small book that can create HUGE results in your life. Clearly, you're a person who won't cheat yourself by *dabbling*. For that, I salute you and give you my deepest respect.

How do you want to be remembered? I believe one of the greatest gifts that all human has is the ability to make decisions. Everything that has ever happened to us, we have the ability to decide what it means for us. For many, life is nothing but a boring bus ride. For some, life is like a crazy roller coaster that gives us many moment that takes our breath away and our minds off!

I hope that we'll stay connected and you'll write an email to tell me how this book helped or served you. In the future, I'll be writing more books, giving out more free content and creating more powerful online courses and classes.

Till then, remember to claim your free bonus, remain positive and expect amazing miracles to happen in your life… because *you* are one.

"Go for it now. The future is promised to no one"
— Wayne Dyer

CPSIA information can be obtained
at www.ICGtesting.com
Printed in the USA
BVHW030246300519
549345BV00042B/855/P